# Say Goodbye To Stuttering!

## Practical Anti-Stuttering Solutions

Suzzie Santos

Copyright © 2015 ***Suzzie Santos***

All rights reserved.

*No part of this book may be reproduced or transmitted in any form whatsoever, electronic, or mechanical, including photocopying, recording, or by any informational storage or retrieval system without express permission from the author.*

Copyright © 2015 ***Suzzie Santos***

All rights reserved.

ISBN-13:
978-1519777836

ISBN-10:
1519777833

## Basic Techniques To Control Stutter

Stuttering, also known as stammering is a speech disorder in which the normal flow of speech is often interrupted by repeating of noises, syllables, words or phrases, pauses and prolongations that vary both in frequency and severity from those of a generally fluent speaker.

The term stuttering is connected with spontaneous sound repetition. An example of uncontrolled sound repetition, would be:

- Trying to say the word "ken", but instead saying "k-k-ken".

Many times these individuals will put words together. An example would be:.

- "Lllllets g-g-go home".

Not just is stammering spontaneous sound repeating, it likewise includes the abnormal reluctance or stopping briefly before speaking. This time out or doubt is typically called a "block".

A lot of the variables that comprise 'true' stuttering cannot be heard or seen by a listener. The important things that cannot be observed consist of:

Anxiety, shame, "loss of control", sensations felt throughout the speech, situational worries and tension.

Typically, the toughest element of the stutter or stammering condition is the emotional state of the individual. A greater rate of stuttering has been observed in African and West Indian adults. Males around the world make up about eighty percent of all stutterers.
Presently, there is no recognized cause for the disorder. There are a number of theories for the condition; they can be divided into 3 categories.
'The "Monster" study', 'Genetics', and 'Childhood development'.

Quick Facts:
- Stutters can develop later on in life, but are triggered through a stroke or other brain injury.
- Stuttering starts in early youth, when a child was initially developing his or her speech and language abilities. - The bulk of stutters develop in between the ages of 2 and 5. - 50 % to 70 % of all stutterers are related to another stutterer. - Most kids go through a stage of disfluency in early speech.

When a person develops a stutter or parents understand that their kid is forming a stutter, they want to learn the cause. It can be troubling and worrying to the child and their moms and dads. So what triggers a stutter?

These are some of them:
An over aggressive relative. It can be a distressing event. People might copy a mate at school who has a stutter and then it sticks. It can run in the family.

Not all who stutter have it from an early age. Many individuals who stutter have a father and mother or relative who has a stutter and they have picked up their stuttering practice potentially from this individual.
Stuttering is an awkward problem. You may be so embarrassed by your speech that you speak as little as possible.

If stuttering has been a problem for you, do not give up hope-- there are solutions! You can learn how to take control of your speech, instead of permitting it to manage you!

There are simple techniques to help control your stuttering. When you attempt these methods, you will learn which ones work the best. You can then start to use them on your everyday speech.

Mastering the simple techniques to manage your stutter can do wonders for your self-confidence. When you learn of the art of interacting smoothly, it will enhance your confidence in your daily life.

Some individuals require a little extra assistance to manage their stuttering. Often there are unique situations which require a unique approach, in order to work. Whichever classification describes you, or a relative who stutters, they are all attended to in this book.

For many individuals who stutter, mastering some basic techniques is all they need to do. Stuttering does not have to ever be a problem just as before. You may need to use a number of strategies to have reliable speech. Whether your stuttering is serious or slight, you cannot pick up total control over your stutter overnight however.

## Think About What You Wish to Convey

There is more to speech than simply saying words. When you speak to someone, you are trying to communicate something. Possibly you are trying to clarify something, get a point across or ask a question. Whenever you speak, there is a message in what you are saying. Thinking of what you wish to communicate

beforehand has advantages which can help you to manage your stuttering.
What do you want to say, and what do you hope the listener will pick up from it? It just takes a few minutes to contemplate on these elements before you start to speak.
Thinking of what you want to convey places strength behind your message. It can also place strength behind your speech. The way this is done, is it puts your focus on the importance of what you are saying-- why it is essential. This focus can, in turn, divert your self-consciousness far from your speech. It may even remove it entirely.

Instead of just saying words, you will be communicating your state of mind, attitude, and the confidence which accompanies it. You will be speaking plainly, instead of safe-guarding your speech. With practice, this method can assist you to control your stutter.

## Making and Maintaining Eye Contact

The person who stutters develops the habit of avoiding eye contact with the people to whom he is speaking. He has become so accustomed to his stuttering speech that he does not want to see the response of the listener. This can cause you to become even more uncomfortable, and stutter even more.

You can turn this unfavorable habit around to your favor. While it may take some practice, it is well-worth the effort. When you are preparing to talk with someone, make a point of making eye contact with him. You can begin by advising yourself that he truly does want to hear whatever you say. You will receive a spoken or unspoken affirmation of this, before beginning to speak.
As you speak, hold eye contact with that person. If you speak pleasantly, and reflect this pleasant attitude in the eye contact rather than a bold stare, you will see that he is listening happily to whatever you are saying to him.

This technique can help you to develop the habit of appreciating one-on-one communication. It can assist you to focus on the interaction itself, instead of on your speech trouble. You will gain control over your spoken communications, and find them to be more satisfying. As these routines begin to come naturally, your speech will likewise start to flow more naturally.

## Learning and Applying Deep Breathing to Your Speech

Appropriate breathing can play a considerable role in controlling your stutter. It is an excellent, healthy routine which you can find by yourself, and put into practical use.

Doing this in a calm, peaceful environment where you will not be disturbed by other people or outside sound is more suitable. Exercise this simple, deep breathing strategy up to two times a day-- until it feels natural.

It can boost your self-esteem if you practice this strategy on inanimate things, or your pet. Do the deep breathing technique before speaking, and briefly during your "conversation.".
When your focus is taken off your speech and focused on your breathing, you will feel much more positive when you are speaking. It unwinds all of the muscles that you use when you are speaking, helping your speech to flow smoothly.

After you have uncovered ways to do this, you can attempt it on people. It is very important to keep in mind that after you have mastered this habit, the individual you are speaking to will most likely not even notice you are doing it. Your speech will be much more purposeful, well-thought, and lesser possibility of stuttering.

## Develop a Great Sense of Humor

If you stutter, you understand this. Even when you start learning how to control your stutter, you may periodically commit mistakes. This is especially true if you have been ridiculed about your stuttering in the past. A sense of humor about your stutter is the healthiest method to battle it.

Think about situations you have remained in, when your stutter was specifically annoying. Think about how much better the eventual outcome might have been, if you had had the ability to laugh and make a joke of it. It would not have seemed so terrible wouldn't it?

Next, think of how you can integrate a sense of humor into future stuttering. Perhaps you can consider it in the exact same terms as an unscripted bout of hiccups. If a hiccup would not lead you to becoming ashamed and flustered, neither should a stutter!

Acknowledging the possibility of a mistake, makes it less likely for one to in fact take place. You will not fret about stuttering, and spoken communication will be more pleasurable for yourself and for everyone else concerned.

## Calm Your Nerves

If you think about your history with stuttering, you may see just how much more of a problem it was whenever you were nervous. When you fidget, you become self-conscious; when you are uneasy, you are less in control. It can become a vicious circle of nervousness, self-consciousness, and loss of control over your stuttering.

Keeping yourself calm takes effort and practice. If you fidget by nature, or if your everyday life contains situations that provoke nervousness, it might take even more effort.

The more calm you are able to stay on a regular basis, the more control you will have over your stutter. As stuttering and stammering can be directly related to anxiousness -- working on this problem can decrease your stuttering and offer you more control. Teaching yourself to adopt a calm disposition and a favorable outlook may not remove your stuttering, however it can help to lower it.

In addition to these aspects, certain products which you take in can also contribute to nervousness. Caffeine is one of the offenders. If you have the habit of consuming servings of coffee, tea, or soft drinks during the day, switching to much healthier, non-caffeinated beverages will be useful. The shakiness you feel after a large quantity of caffeine can affect every part of your body, including the muscles which are employed during speech. Giving up this product or reducing your consumption can be beneficial.

Some individuals have a similar reaction to sugar. While this is not true for everyone, it deserves examining if you have a stuttering problem. Decreasing the quantity of sugar in your diet might assist you to become calmer. You can try it, and see if it works for you!

## Is Avoidance a Useful Technique?

Avoidance is a controversial problem. Some people insist it works well, while others do not find it as handy. The debate is in whether avoidance is a suitable technique for controlling a stuttering problem. If you only care about techniques that work, it is a good idea to ignore the controversy and just try it on your own.

The basic way avoidance is practiced is to substitute words that are simple to speak in place of those which are not. If you have been bothered by your stuttering to the level of reading this book, you are probably knowledgeable on the distinction. You would find that a large number of words appear to flow rather quickly, while others become "stuck" or wants to be repeated. You might have likewise seen that particular sounds, or specific letters of the alphabet, are more annoying than others.

When you are considering this strategy, you may wish to look at both sides of the matter. Exercising avoidance can help you to feel more in control of your speech. Avoidance can also have negative ramifications. When you approach speaking to somebody in this manner, you might wind up being more uneasy. This can backfire; for others, it is not a problem at all.

If you want to give this technique a try, put a little time into the "demons" of your speech.

When you know which words, sounds, and letters are usually at fault for triggering a stutter, you can choose a different word that suggests the same thing. You will find that language is a fantastic thing indeed-- there is a synonym, or a related word, for each word you wish to say! If the word "box" is one of your speech demons, attempt saying "container" instead. You can expand your vocabulary, while learning a new strategy to control stutter.

## Practice of Speaking Slowly

You may currently know that when your words come out in an out of breath rush, it makes your stutter even worse. You start to say a word, and many other words seem to tumble after, like a domino-effect. Developing the practice of speaking slowly is a method which can assist you to control your stutter.

Learning how to speak gradually is not tough. If you have not yet cultivated this practice, now is a good time to begin. When you wish to speak, take a minute to prepare yourself. Form each word slowly, and allow each word to flow effortlessly and naturally. Rather than being in a hurry to get a full sentence out, consider each word as flowing from you to your listener.

When you notice that the other person is listening to whatever you are saying, this can help you to speak gradually. It is better than merely exchanging words, or waiting for your opportunity to speak.

Equally essential, if you contemplate on this when you are preparing to have a conversation with somebody; it can help you to control your stutter. As your words flow smoothly and steadily, you will see how it benefits your speech.

## How Relaxation Can Help Control Stutter

Relaxation has a dual function in managing stuttering. It works on both the body and the mind.

First, relaxation influences every part of your body-- your entire system. This consists of all of the muscles that are made use of when you speak. From the muscles in your throat to that diaphragm, the more relaxed your body is, the simpler the words will flow. Relaxed muscles mean smoother speech; and smoother speech implies less chance of stuttering.

Second, relaxation influences the mind. Even if you currently know this, you may not have thought of how it is linked to your speech. The mind that is relaxed is much better focused and more regulated. It is less bothered by slight annoyances which develop uneasiness, stress, and self-consciousness. In turn, when the mind is relaxed and at ease, you are less likely to experience stuttering.

It is not difficult, even if you have a busy way of life. You can begin with sluggish, deep breathing.

After you have learned how to do this, you can take your brand-new practice with you when you need to communicate with other people. Before that, visualize a calm environment. Allow the soothing relaxation to fill your mind, and to fill your body. Not only will you feel more at ease, even in business or social situations, your mind and body will savor the results of relaxation, and will help manage your stutter.

## Develop Confidence in Your Speech

The more confident you are, the less problem you will have with stuttering. If you have been

bothered by stammering for a long time, it might take time and effort to develop this confidence.
The more worthy and important you understand you are as an individual, the simpler it will be to develop confidence in yourself. Even if you are naturally shy, this can help you to become more assertive.

Developing self-confidence in your speech can be just as easy. This means that even if you are not yet sure of yourself, when you speak as if you do-- it will become a truth.

Tell yourself that you are knowledgeable about the subject you are speaking about, and that it is important for you to say it. Let your words flow, with the same air of authority and confidence. While exercising the breathing method you have already learned, speak without stopping briefly on individual words.

When you have demonstrated this self-confidence, you will be less likely to falter on those bothersome words. With practice, your stutter may become a distant memory.

## Does Analyzing Help or Make Stuttering Worse?

You may have heard of analyzing. You might have attempted it yourself. The truth is, in numerous cases it can in fact aggravate stuttering. While this book is offering you with practical techniques to manage your stutter, keep in mind that this conventional practice is hardly ever in a stutterer's best interest. Analyzing is typically done by putting time and effort into attempting to determine the problem, in hopes of alleviating it. Assessing can consist of studying the vocabulary one makes use of regularly, seeking those pesky "devil" words. It can likewise include taking unique note of the parts of one's body and muscles one uses during daily speech.

The negative element of examining in this manner is it highlights the problem, rather than useful options. You may end up so alert to troublesome words, that it promotes your stuttering. You may become so concentrated on your muscles that it prevents your capability to speak clearly. You can become so uneasy that your stuttering gets worse.

Your goal must be to control stutter, to communicate effectively. Placing too much emphasis on your stutter is not the best way. Rather than dwelling in the problems, you will be living in the solution-- making the most of all of your verbal interactions!

## Can Medications Help?

You may be at wit's end over your stuttering. Maybe discontent or fear is getting in the way of managing your stutter.

An excellent general rule is to rule out medication unless your stuttering is so serious that natural methods do not help. While some people might disagree, any kind of medication for stammering needs to be considered only as a last resort. Unless your stuttering is due to a medical problem which requires your doctor's evaluation and instructions. Depending on natural methods is much better than counting on pharmaceuticals.

If you are considering medication, it is crucial for you to seek your doctor's advice. Under no circumstances should you ever attempt to self-medicate. Making use of any sort of pharmaceutical item without your medical professional's approval can be hazardous. You desire relief from your stutter, but taking too many chances with your health is never the right option.

This chapter will provide you an introduction of the medications which are typically used to alleviate or control stuttering. If you are thinking of trying medication to manage your stutter, your medical professional can advise a medication for you. You may also seek another physician who is more open to alternative methods of therapies. Let your OTHER medical professional deal or make compatible conflicting therapies.

Zyprexa has a moderate success rate in dealing with stuttering. This drug is mainly used for dealing with schizophrenia and other comparable conditions. The experiences of people who have used Zyprexa for stuttering range from a high degree of satisfaction to no effect at all. Zyprexa is a dopamine-blocker drug. Its side effects can vary from lessening alertness to weight gain.

There are a variety of medical conditions which contraindicates the use of Zyprexa, so it must never be put to use without your physician having full understanding of your case history. A lesser-known fact about Zyprexa is that its tablet contains aspartame, making it unsafe for patients who have phenylketonuria (known as PKU).

While some medical professionals disagree with the practice of prescribing tranquilizers for stuttering, others think that they can be useful. The general agreement amongst those who consider it an appropriate form of treatment is that lowering the individual's anxiety and nervousness will, in turn, decrease his stuttering.

The possible side effects of tranquilizers can range from minor to severe; an added element is it can lead to addiction. Dependency to tranquilizers and withdrawal from these drugs is typically difficult and uncomfortable. If your physician feels that this is the ideal form of treatment for you, your use of tranquilizers must be thoroughly kept an eye on.

Some physicians believe that antidepressants can support to alleviate stuttering. Studies have revealed that while some individuals do get relief from this kind of treatment, others experience worse stuttering than they had before the treatment. As is the problem with any pharmaceutical preparation, making use of antidepressants should be decided on a case-

to-case basis. Even with your case history in hand, your doctor may not have the ability to figure out beforehand whether these drugs will assist you or whether your stuttering will become worse.
While the side results of antidepressants can vary from sleep disruptions to sexual difficulties and others, the side effects a person has from antidepressants is mainly based on his own experiences. Some find the side effects to be just moderately bothersome, while others consider the side effect more excruciating than the preliminary problem.

2 drugs currently on the market which show a substantial promise in dealing with stuttering are Haldol and Risperdal. Both of these are dopamine-blockers. While they both have the capacity of triggering serious side-effects in some patients, research have revealed these medications to have as much as fifty-percent success rate in treating stuttering.
Plenty of physicians concur that dopamine-blocking drugs are the approach of choice when utilizing medication to treat stuttering, but as this has not continued to be in practice for long, it is smart to take a look at the ramifications of this before going the medication path.

You want relief from your stutter? You might be willing to go to any lengths to be free of the problem right? For the sake of both your short-term and long-term health, you should not be too quick to decide that drugs are the answer. As any pharmaceutical preparation has the potential to cause complications, you need to plainly evaluate both the advantages and the risks. You should likewise seek the guidance of a qualified doctor.

The most sensible approach to making use of medication for the treatment of stuttering is to think about it just as a last resort. Unless all the natural techniques for controlling your stutter have failed, and you have found that your stuttering disrupts your life that you cannot handle it.

Many are too rash to consider drugs as quick, miracle-cures. They do not understand how hazardous drugs can be to their health. Some medical professionals also have the viewpoint that medication is the best course of action -- without even examining all of the alternatives!

## Special Needs: Stuttering in Kids

While many of the methods explained in this book are similarly suitable for youngsters, the child who stutters may have special needs which likewise must be resolved.

A child who stammers remains in an especially-vulnerable position. Whether he is a young child or a teen, stuttering can have worse impact than what an adult experiences.

The most significant result stuttering has on a youngster is in his relations with other people, especially his peers. A speech obstacle like stuttering can impede a child capability to connect with his peers.

This problem can make it much more tough for the child to make friends. It is not unusual for a child who stutters to become separated and depressed. His self-confidence can be much lower than that of a non-stuttering youngster; he may develop an unfavorable opinion of himself.

These concerns are why stuttering should be addressed as soon as you recognize it in your youngster. The quicker you begin to help him to control his stutter, the better his general quality of life will be. Oftentimes, stuttering is noticeable long before a child begins school. In other circumstances, it is not evident till he is older.

Building your child's self-esteem goes hand in hand with helping him to manage his stutter. While it needs to be obvious, fathers and mothers and other adults should never ever make the error of shaming a child about his stuttering. The more of a problem you make about his stuttering, the worse he will feel about himself. This, in turn, can result in his stuttering worsening. He might feel that he is to blame for his problem, which will just intensify it.
While adults might not be harmed by making a joke on stuttering, this is hardly ever the case for kids. Even the most well-meaning siblings can suppress a child progress in managing a stutter by making "jokes" about it. It is no laughing matter to the child who stutters. Sarcasm and jokes can be devastating to the child.

The kid who stammers needs to know that you and the other people in his life are supporting. He has to understand that he is not turned down, nor looked down on, over his problem. He needs to understand that he is accepted and loved, as he is-- stuttering included. This sort of unconditional love and approval will supply a strong foundation for helping him to manage his stutter without the child seeing the problem as a reflection of himself.

Providing a calm environment is the very best way to begin supporting your child to control his stutter. Many of the methods explained in this book can also be presented as games. Instead of presenting a technique as something which he have to perform in order to overcome a problem, enabling him to view a method as fun and enjoyable will produce the best results.

Teaching youngster techniques to help him manage his stutter can be a little more painful and aggravating for the adult than it is for the child. He might not be cooperative; or you might not see any clear outcomes. It is vital for you to not be demanding, or require him to practice a specific strategy constantly. It is likewise essential for you to not communicate your aggravation when you think a technique is ineffective. Both of these mistakes can quickly backfire. They can cause him to give up.

Persuading your child that learning techniques to manage his stutter is something which he in fact wants to do, is not as tough as it might sound. A lot of moms and dads have practice in encouraging their youngsters that certain things are a great idea. When approaches of managing stuttering are presented in a light-hearted, fun way, your child will usually comply just because he wishes to comply.

While parents might think that rewarding a child for learning an approach is a favorable technique, it typically is not. If your kid becomes accustomed to perks, this can make it even harder for him when he is not effective. He might even feel that he is being penalized for slipping up. When learning ways to manage a stutter, errors are as common in children as they are in adults. Just letting him understand that you appreciate his efforts, no matter the results, is much better than providing him rewards. A child will be eager to develop a new ability when he sees that his efforts are valued.

When parents notice their kid stuttering, they often panic. This can mean rushing him to his pediatrician, making consultations to see speech therapists, and even considering medication. You can save both yourself and your child from a great deal of unnecessary aggravation by not being too quick to conclude that he will be a long term stutterer without immediate intervention.

The fact is that children stutter at times. Some young children stutter when they are at first learning verbal abilities; others stutter when they are very nervous, worn out, or feel overloaded. In the interest of your child's emotional health, you must withstand seeing these kinds of scenarios as potentially-serious problems. If you are your child's main caretaker, it must not be difficult to figure out whether he is displaying a speech impediment or just a phase.

Talking on the problem of stuttering in youngsters likewise includes the factor of medication. As parents are typically not experienced about this, it has to be noted that some medications which are given to children can cause them to stutter, even when they don't have a real speech impediment.

Ritalin, which is prescribed for such conditions as ADHD and ADD, is one of the most common culprits. If you notice stuttering in a child who is taking this or other medications, it needs to be brought to the attention of his medical professional. The medication may be the cause of his stuttering. If so, adjusting the dose or changing medications can eliminate his stuttering totally. However, this ought to not be tried without your doctor's recommendation.

The child who stutters is just as typical as other kids. The way he is treated in his daily life needs to emphasize this fact. Stuttering can be unsafe to a child's self-confidence and social growth; it is not nearly as unsafe as making a problem of the problem. The child, who knows that he is loved and accepted as he is, while being offered techniques to assist him manage his stutter in the most satisfying manner possible, is the child who is more than likely to be successful.

**Speech Therapist Necessary?**

Whether you are trying to find assistance for yourself or for your child, you might be thinking about requesting assistance from a speech therapist. You might wonder if this is the right choice. There are a number of points to consider when deciding if you or your child needs to see a speech therapist.

One a circumstance in which speaking with a speech therapist is a legitimate technique is if stuttering is so extreme that it impacts your performance. If it is so extreme that it is disruptive to your everyday life, help from an expert may be in order. Whether the stuttering has been a long-term problem, or whether its beginning has been abrupt, a speech therapist can be practical.

A second scenario is if all strategies and techniques for controlling your stutter have failed. Although the methods explained in this book are easy to learn and successful for many people, they may not be as efficient for you. If you have put your best effort into these strategies, and have found no relief from your stuttering, a visit to a speech therapist may help.

Another situation makings a speech therapist a wise decision is if your stuttering is associated with any medical or psychological cause. In these circumstances, managing your stutter on your own may be impossible. If a preexisting medical or mental condition is found to be at the root of your stutter, a speech therapist can direct you to the expert aid that is appropriate for you.

The youngster whose stutter is so severe that no strategies supply any relief is one of these scenarios. The youngster whose stutter places an unnecessary concern on his daily life is another.

The child who chooses not to work together in finding how to manage his stutter is another scenario which requires a speech therapist. This does not mean rushing making a consultation as quickly as your child refuses to comply.
You need to expect some degree of dullness or disinterest when teaching him these new ideas. The youngster who flatly refuses to work together at all, shows anger or resentment at your attempts to aid, or securely believes that nothing will work, can benefit from seeing a speech therapist. The youngster who displays mental problems connected with his stutter can likewise gain from seeing an expert in these instances, his pediatrician or your family physician can advise a therapist who can help him.

If you or your kid will be seeing a speech therapist, these visits must not be disruptive to everyday life than needed. The kid who sees a therapist may resent putting his time into it, and might feel that this strategy is a negative reflection on himself. The best technique for dealing with these concerns is to present the visits in a positive light. If he views his speech therapist as a friend, and as a good person who truly wants to assist him, he can look forward to the visits and take advantage of them much more.

Speech therapists can be expensive. You can check to see if your insurance will cover a speech therapist, or ask if he or she will accept a reasonable payment plan.

Your doctor or family physician is the best resource for locating a speech therapist. He knows your particular situation, and can advise the therapist who corrects for you. Does not hesitate in requesting for his recommendations.

In most cases, stuttering can be managed solely by learning these basic techniques and applying them to your daily speech. But, if you or your child is in one of these special circumstances, a professional speech therapist can be greatly useful. The faster you request for aid, the quicker you can get the stutter under control.
Progress, Not Perfection

Whenever you are learning something brand-new, success does not come instantaneously. Anticipating overnight results, or anticipating excellence, are a recipe for catastrophe. This is among the most vital indicators to bear in mind when you are learning how to manage your stutter.

Expecting too much, too quickly, or expecting that you will never stutter again, positions too much pressure on yourself. You need to avoid this kind of pressure if you truly intend to succeed!

When you consider control of your stutter in regards to learning a brand-new skill, both the results and your frame of mind will be far better. As learning anything new requires time, practice, and even trial-and-error, this is likewise the case with learning how to control your stutter. Some strategies will work much better for you than others; some techniques will not work for you; and others will grant impressive results. If you are willing to make the commitment, you can achieve success.

Perseverance is the needed key in learning to manage your stutter. You should be prepared to put your time into learning a strategy, and applying it to your everyday conversations.

Progress is not a warranty of excellence. Even after you have mastered a technique and put it into practice, you might still experience a mistake. You might have felt that you were completely free of your stutter, just to have it happen at the most bothersome time. Instead of becoming flustered, or stressing that you have not accomplished anything, lightheartedly brushing it off is a far better method.
The idea of "development- not perfection" is more valid for the child who stammers. As youngsters are more naturally inclined to view a minor setback or mistake as a full disaster, teaching him to see his achievements for how outstanding they are is the most beneficial strategy.

You can begin by instilling this concept before you start to teach him the methods to control his stutter. Absolutely nothing genuinely worthwhile was ever achieved overnight; and even in the very best conditions, mistakes do take place. When he is equipped with these principles before he begins to learn the techniques, he is prepared for success and will appreciate it every step of the way.

Stammering does not need to play a huge role in your life. It does not need to interfere with your communications with other people, nor impact the way you take a look at yourself. All it takes is time, effort, and commitment to learn these easy methods. When you see which strategies work best for you, practicing them will give you an optimistic view of your ability to speak clearly in social situations. Applying them regularly whenever you communicate verbally with other people will supply you with more self-confidence than you have ever had before.

Learning how to control your stutter is your first step to a happier, more satisfying life. The more you practice, the more development you will make-- and this is the very definition of true success!

Stuttering Courses

During the first few days of the course, the stutter speech coach describes the strategies which are needed to overcome the stutter. The first day is usually the most crucial day. This is the client's easy day, as the coach will do the majority of the talking; discussing in detail half of the speech policies needed to beat the stutter. They are most likely going to ask the client to discuss their history, consisting of details about how their stutter started, about their household, about their interests, plus any other facts they would like to reveal.

On the 2nd day the client becomes more involved, beginning to put into practice what they have learned from the previous day. The final speech rules are taught on this day.
The final three days are invested practicing, enabling the guidelines to become embedded as a natural part of the client's speech.
Some of the areas in the courses might be:
- Why people stutter
- Public speaking strategy
- Interview strategy
- Telephone technique
The speech guidelines:
The individual who has a stutter should not fret about the contents of the stutter course. If there is an area of the course that they would rather not cover, it will be respected.
Each course is special; as every stutterer is different this is why courses are usually worked on a one-to-one basis.

People have the ability to keep in contact after the course through email and telephone which acts as a back up and continued long term support.

Other books:

**Available at fine online book retailers everywhere.**

1 De-Clutter Your World, Declutter Your Life
"Clearing Crap, One Day At A Time..."
Trevor Hawkins

2 Addiction Crash Course In One Sitting
Liberate Yourself From All Addictions!
Trevor Hawkins

3 Apnea No More!
Easy Ways Out Of Sleep Apnea
Trevor Hawkins

4 Handling Aspergers
Crucial Treatment Options For Asperger's Syndrome
Suzzie Santos

5 Engineering & Raising Children Who Succeed!
"Why Succesful Kids Are Made, Not Born"
Suzzie Santos

6 The Beginner's Comedy Manual
Mastering The Finer Points Of The Craft
Samantha Humphries

7 Mastering Family Finances
The Family Budgeting Crash Course
Suzzie Santos

8 Learning Gratitude In One Sitting
How To Improve Your Life Through Thankfulness
Trevor Hawkins

9 Zero To Hero Real Estate
A Crash Course On Real Estate Fundamentals
Aiden Sisko

10 Mastering Rejections In One Sitting
How To Enjoy & Benefit From Rejections!
Trevor Hawkins

11 The Ins And Outs Of Developing Self-Confidence
Learn Self Confidence In One Sitting
Trevor Hawkins

12 Spirituality In One Sitting
Learn Fundamental Mystical & Spiritual Practices
Trevor Hawkins

Made in the USA
Las Vegas, NV
09 July 2022